Cool Tools

by Alison Auch

Content and Reading Adviser: Joan Stewart
Educational Consultant/Literacy Specialist
New York Public Schools

Spyglass
BOOKS

COMPASS POINT BOOKS

Minneapolis, Minnesota

Compass Point Books
3722 West 50th Street, #115
Minneapolis, MN 55410

Visit Compass Point Books on the Internet at *www.compasspointbooks.com*
or e-mail your request to *custserv@compasspointbooks.com*

Photographs © Two Coyote Studios/Mary Walker Foley.

Project Manager: Rebecca Weber McEwen
Editor: Jennifer Waters
Photo Researcher: Jennifer Waters
Photo Selectors: Rebecca Weber McEwen and Jennifer Waters
Designer: Mary Walker Foley

Library of Congress Cataloging-in-Publication Data

Auch, Alison.
  Cool tools / by Alison Auch.
     p. cm. -- (Spyglass books)
  ISBN 0-7565-0230-6 (hardcover)
  1. Simple machines--Juvenile literature. [1. Simple machines.] I.
Title. II. Series.
  TJ147 .A87 2002
  621.8--dc21
                              2001007321

Contents

What Is a Machine?

A machine is an object
that does work.
Some machines may be
so simple that you do not
even know you are using
a machine!

The stapler, the staple remover, the scissors, and the hole punch are simple machines.

Scissors

A pair of scissors is a simple machine!

This cool tool helps us cut paper, hair, cloth, or food. It is really just two knife **blades** attached by a screw.

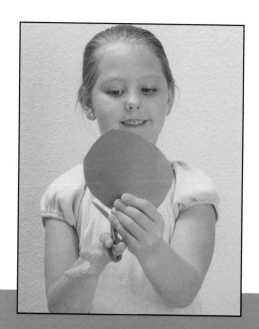

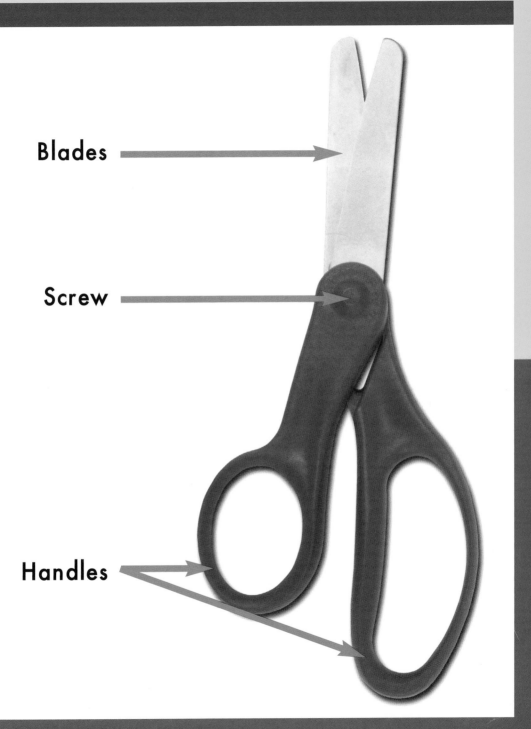

Blades

Screw

Handles

Doorknob

A doorknob is
a simple machine!

A doorknob makes it easier
for us to open and
lock our doors.

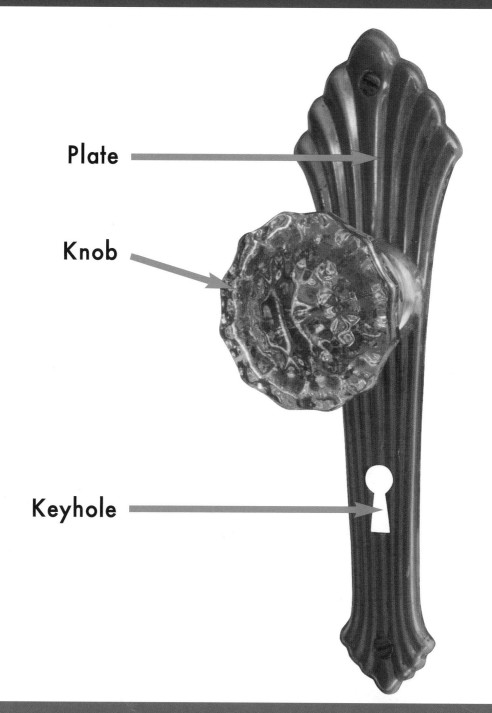

Plate

Knob

Keyhole

Toilet

A toilet is a simple machine!

A toilet is important
in our daily lives. Long ago,
people did not have toilets.
They went outside or
used *chamber pots*.

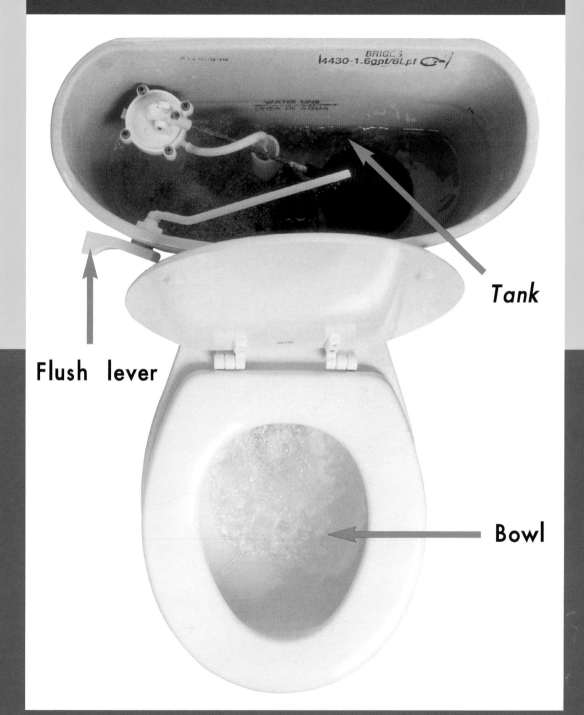

Tank

Flush lever

Bowl

Can Opener

A can opener is
a simple machine!

We use this cool tool
to open cans of food.
It is hard to open a can
without one!

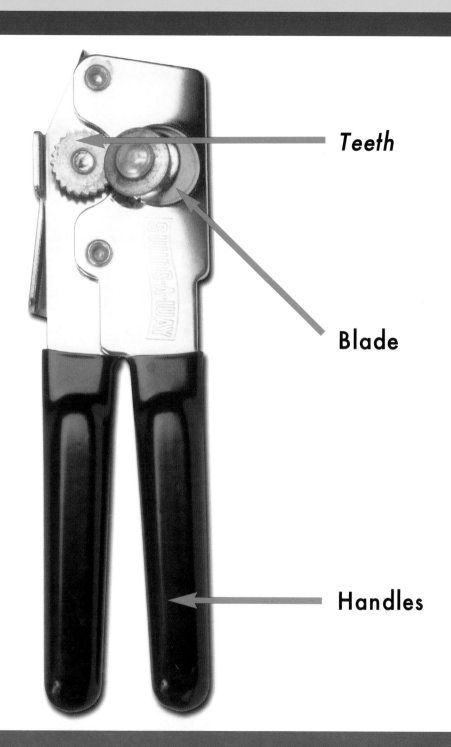

Teeth

Blade

Handles

Clothespin

A clothespin is
a simple machine!

This cool tool keeps
people's clean clothes
attached to clotheslines and
off the dirty ground!

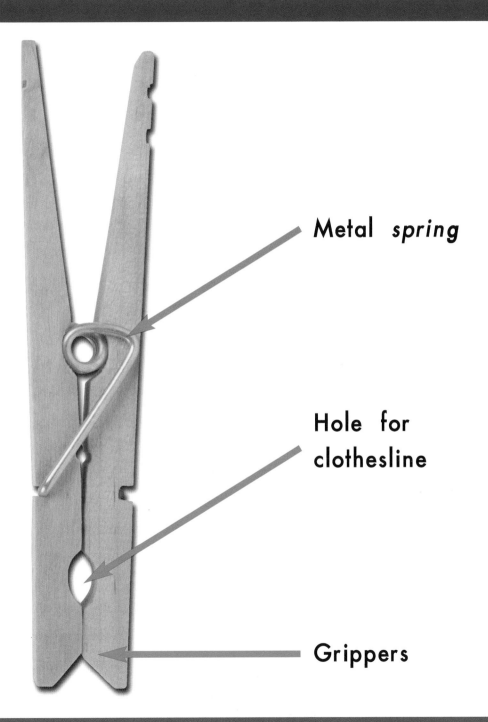

Metal *spring*

Hole for
clothesline

Grippers

15

Pliers

A pair of pliers is a simple machine!

This cool tool helps hold and bend things, such as wire, that are hard to bend with our bare hands.

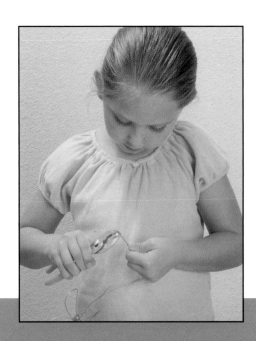

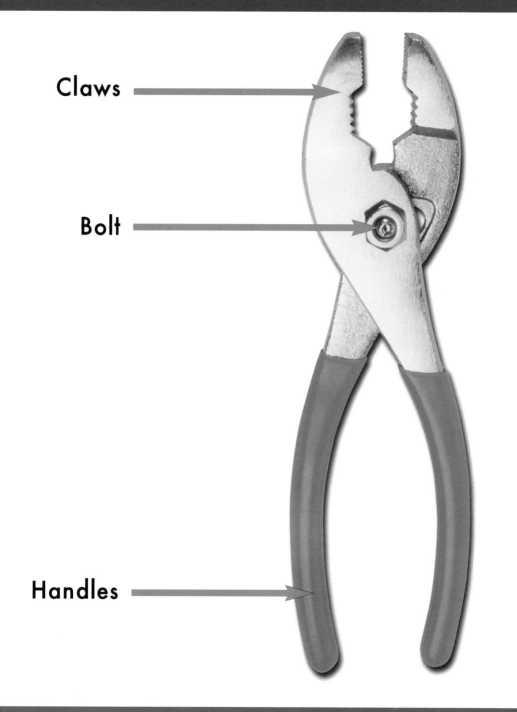

Claws

Bolt

Handles

Pizza Cutter

A pizza cutter is
a simple machine!

This cool tool makes quick
and safe cuts in a pizza.
Without pizza cutters,
we would have to wait longer
to eat our pizza!

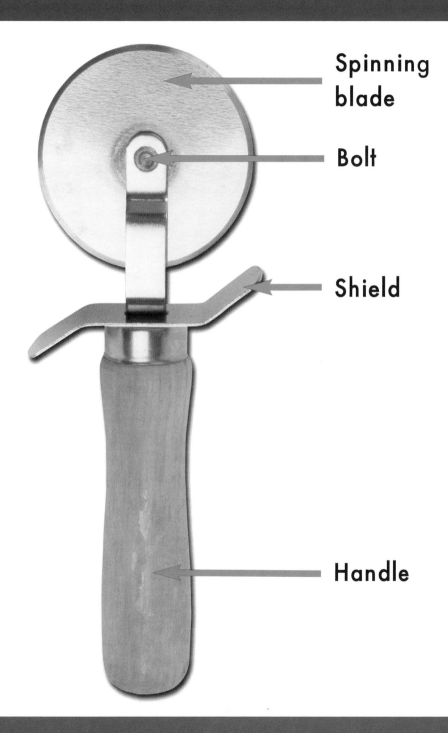

Spinning
blade

Bolt

Shield

Handle

Fun Facts

A man named
Sir Thomas Crapper
built the first modern
toilet in the 1860s.

Pizza is the
Italian word for
"pie." When you
cut a pizza, you
usually cut it just
like you would
a pie.

Some of the very first tools
made by people were machines.
One rock hitting another
to sharpen it was a machine.

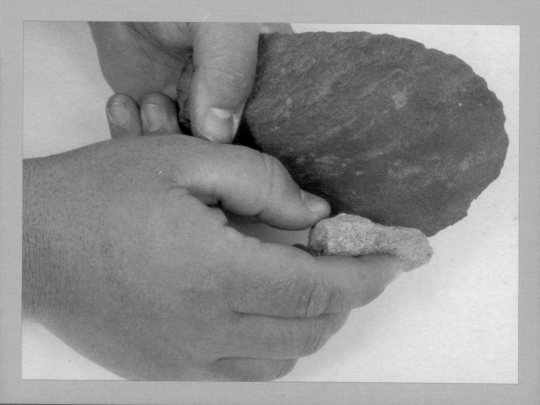

Glossary

blade—a sharp, cutting part of a piece of metal

chamber pot—a type of bowl that people used as a toilet

spring—a metal spiral that goes back to its original shape after being stretched or pulled

tank—a large container, often used to store water

teeth—pieces of metal sticking out around the edges of a wheel

Learn More

Books

Fowler, Allan. *What Magnets Can Do*. Chicago: Childrens Press, 1995.

Gibbons, Gail. *Clocks and How They Go*. New York: Thomas Y. Crowell, 1979.

Morris, Ann. *Tools*. Photographs by Ken Heyman. New York: Lothrop, Lee & Shepard Books, 1992.

Web Sites

National Geographic
www.nationalgeographic.com/features/96/inventions

PBS Kids
www.pbs.org/wgbh/aso/tryit/tech/

Index

GR: G
Word Count: 205

From Alison Auch

Reading and writing are my favorite things to do. When I'm not reading or writing, I like to hike in the mountains or play with my five cats!